Sally Petch lives in rural West Sussex overlooking a
churchyard. As well as writing, she runs a reflexology
and Flower Essence practice. She is passionate about
wildlife, drawing and walking beach labyrinths, and
mugs of Assam tea. She can be contacted via her website
www.deathmatters.co.uk

Also by Sally Petch

Gordon's Gifts

Death Matters

Sally Petch

Matador

9 Priory Business Park,
Wistow Road, Kibworth Beauchamp,
Leicestershire. LE8 0RX
Tel: (+44) 116 279 2299
Fax: (+44) 116 279 2277
Email: books@troubador.co.uk
Web: www.troubador.co.uk/matador

ISBN 978 1780883 212

British Library Cataloguing in Publication Data.
A catalogue record for this book is available from the British Library.

Typeset in 11pt Adobe Garamond Pro by Troubador Publishing Ltd, Leicester, UK
Printed and bound in the UK by TJ International, Padstow, Cornwall

Matador is an imprint of Troubador Publishing Ltd

This one is for you SM.
Far ahead of the Indian trackers, halo gleaming softly.

- Death Matters, because twinned with birth, it is universally experienced by every living thing.

- Death Matters is a book filled with thoughts, anecdotes, shared experiences and tasks to help us to accept and feel more comfortable with our own journey towards death.

IN THE early 1960s, I caught pneumonia. I remember my father going out to collect the village doctor who was unable to drive as he had lost his licence due to drink driving. He stood in the hallway after examining me and I heard him tell my mother that that night would be the turning point one way or another. I knew what he meant; death was a possibility, and yet I felt a detachment from fear and also intuitively knew that this wasn't my time to die.

Then in my teens I suffered from pleurisy. I was aware of lying in my bed, fighting for my breath, when suddenly I floated up above my body and looked down upon myself.

I knew something rather strange had happened but I can remember being quite unperturbed and, if anything, the whole experience had been simple and quite pleasurable. I calmly told my sister what had occurred and her reaction was very different to mine!

During a kinesiology session, in my early forties, my therapist, as she was muscle testing, suddenly stated,

"You're not afraid of death and dying at all". This was a pivotal moment because, until that point, I hadn't really given it any consideration. Since then, rather than shunning talk of death and dying, I have found it easy to embrace the concept, and to explore its meaning in respect of my beliefs.

In so doing it has made me very aware that not only do I seem to be in a minority, but that it is a subject which makes people very uncomfortable.

"Death is nothing at all." So begins the famous eulogy by Canon Henry Scott Holland, but I have come to find that it is *just* the opposite for so many people in the Western world. It is everything, and our fear of it stops us from ever really living; as a society we go to great lengths to avoid anything to do with death or dying.

Many of my friends and clients have asked who I think will actually want to read a book about death. Doesn't it make you depressed spending so long writing about such a subject they ask? I can honestly say it doesn't. Death is as much a part of life for me as eating and sleeping, and I have long since lost any fear of openly talking about it, if indeed I ever had any.

As I scan magazine articles, internet features, and catch television adverts it has become clear to me that we are obsessed with remaining youthful in almost every aspect.

"To grow old gracefully" as a statement allows us to admit that we are going to die and it brings us closer to what we are so afraid to face. In fact our fear is sometimes so monumental that I am aware many people shy away from ever looking at death or talking about it until it is too late.

We sanitize it, talking about death in euphemisms like: "He's passed away". We use funeral directors to whisk away our dead, where they are laid out, and dressed in clothes they would have worn when alive. Every last detail is seen to for us so that we can remain apart.

Largely the days have passed when the coffin would remain in the house, when tales would be told around it, when the women of the house or close friends would lay out and wash the body. Death then was a part of life and was treated as such.

Instead we now live in a society that is rich in

consumerism and choice, and it appears unthinkable that we are not able to defeat death, that we can't buy ourselves immortality.

It's certainly not for the want of trying. We spend billions on research into diseases.

Medical expertise and surgical operations to keep us here on Planet Earth are becoming the norm and there is constant discussion as to how to grow the bank of organ donors.

Stem cell research is advancing and the USA has a growing number of people opting for cryogenic freezing.

We are obsessed with saving lives as one day it could be our own which needs attention.

We react strongly to news of deaths or disasters, particularly if the casualty was young.

We call it a tragedy and feel the loss as fear. And then as thankfulness that it wasn't us or a loved one, this time.

But it will be us one day and it will be one of our loved ones or a pet or a neighbour or friend. It is a life certainty.

*****

WITHIN THESE pages are many thoughts and ideas about death and loss. They will act as starting points for discussion, because it is only by talking about death, and in particular our own death, that we will begin to conquer our inherent fear of it and that of our own passing.

There are contributions included from people who have already been touched in some way by death and who have chosen to share their wisdom with you.

There are also reflection points throughout and I would suggest that you keep a journal specifically for recording your thoughts as you work through the book.

The first one is coming up right away.

- What drew you to reading this book? What's going on in your life right now that has made you more receptive to the idea of looking at death as a necessary subject for discussion and reflection?

CONSIDER THIS. Would we not plan a special birthday, an anniversary or a seasonal celebration? Then why do we not plan our own death with as much care and attention to detail? Is the celebration of our life not worthy of such preparation?

- Write in your journal how you feel about this at this moment. If you strongly disagree then that is absolutely fine but try to write down why.

- What have you celebrated recently? What did you do? Who with? Try to describe the occasion in detail.

If you haven't celebrated anything for a long time ask yourself the question "why?"

A gentle and non-challenging starting point is to look at how you, your family and friends celebrate seasonal changes and festivals because they *can* sharpen our awareness and acceptance of endings and beginnings.

Many of us have become detached from the natural world, and also from any form of religious or spiritual beliefs, all of which can help us observe, acknowledge and be comfortable with change, and teach us about ritual and ceremony.

- If you keep a diary or have a calendar then go through it to see how many times over the past year you celebrated a seasonal event or a festival: Christmas, Divali, Halloween, a tree dressing, a visit to a bulb field, organized a picnic for Midsummer, planned a birthday celebration, attended a bar mitzvah or christening, a wedding or a funeral.

All of these involve thought, planning and preparation and we all have customs which have been handed down to us through our spiritual practices or through ancestors.

- Write down one of your precious moments from a past celebration. Try to do this in detail. What made it so special?

"My Father has Alzheimer's and doesn't leave his house. He has always loved classical music and was a lifetime concert goer. His other lifelong love was watching Brighton and Hove Albion play football and I took him right up until his 89th Birthday. For his 90th Birthday we organized a local string quartet to set up in his garden, asked all the family over, made food to share, and requested that the musicians learnt "Sussex by the Sea", which is always played when his team came out onto the pitch.

It was an afternoon of sheer joy and something we will always remember.

It was wonderful to have in our memory banks the knowledge that we had witnessed him totally enthralled by the music and loving that moment, even though he wouldn't remember it the next day."

That was a fairly major celebration but they can be far simpler. Each year on my Mother's birthday I visit a nursery, spend time selecting a plant I feel she would have liked, and then return to plant it in my garden.

If there's no one around I might even sing 'Happy Birthday' to her as I water it in!

Strangely I don't do this to mark her death day, but many people visit gravestones to place flowers at this time. I think it was because my Mother was passionate about celebrating birthdays and it makes me remember her tremendous joy for life.

"I have beautiful roses in my garden, planted by the previous occupant who is now residing across the lane in the graveyard. From the first year I lived here I have cut the first rose in bloom and taken it across to place on her grave. I feel this first one belongs to her. I look forward to this small ritual and it highlights the onset of summer."

It is important that any celebration you are asked to participate in resonates within you and is not just something that you do to keep others happy.

"I don't celebrate internally anymore. Firstly I dislike being the centre of attention.

But I don't want to feel obliged to feel happy about an occasion that I would not have bothered with.

I think that many of the commercially led celebrations like Mother/Father's Day or New Year's Eve are just crude exploitations of a society of shoppers."

- Does this strike a chord with you? Are there celebrations you feel compelled to observe because of other people? Is there a way of discussing this and perhaps working towards sharing something which is meaningful? Record your observations in your journal.

FOOD CAN help us observe seasonal changes, particularly if we grow our own food. Only eating food when it is in season not only makes us appreciate food more, but also makes our bodies aware of the changes. Herbalists will tell you that food eaten in the correct season will help us remain in balance. We have become detached from this principle because we have become used to buying any food item we fancy at any time of the year. But to me strawberries belong to the summer and sprouts to the winter. I like observing the correct food seasons because it means I look forward to the first blueberry and can rejoice in eating the first peas straight from the pod.

- Make a list of five fruits and vegetables you enjoy along with their natural season. If you don't know when they would grow without the use of glasshouses or heat then find out.

Growing your own has become the trendy thing to do. One can't open a magazine or newspaper without reading about growing microgreens on the window ledge or beetroot on balconies, but it does anchor us to the seasons to do so. As does any sort of gardening.

- What is the weather like today, right now as you are reading this? What, if any, vegetables are you growing or planning to grow?

- What are you planning to eat for supper tonight?

Try to organise one meal next week which you have cooked from scratch using only ingredients which are seasonal, and preferably locally grown. If you rely on ready meals then buy or borrow a cook book or look up a recipe on the internet. If you already cook from scratch then why not try a new recipe? If it's summer time then can you add some foraged leaves to a salad?

Make sure you are confident about what you are picking. Nettle soup is not only delicious, but free, and packed full of goodness. If this appeals to you then access a foraging course or catch a Ray Mears documentary. Now he really is someone you'd like by you in the event of a disaster!

If it's autumn time how about picking some blackberries and making a fruit crumble? Learning where our food comes from, what it looks like when it is growing, when the natural time to harvest is and how to cook it allows one into the wonder of seasonal appreciation.

It also brings into our consciousness the knowledge that all life is cyclic; that there is a time to lie dormant, a time to grow, and a time to die.

BEGIN TO look at ways of creating ceremony in your life. It may be that you decide to lay the table and sit down to eat formally rather than in front of the television.

It is just so easy to rush from task to task during our days and I think it is good practice to introduce 'Pause Points'. These are times when we can consciously take stock, even if it is only for a few seconds, and to really be present in the moment.

Sharing food lends itself to this. "Breaking of bread" has a deep spiritual significance and just because we are eating pizza does not mean that we should not honour the life-giving food we are about to consume, as well as expressing gratitude to the farmers, cooks, delivery men and shopkeepers who have played their part in our sustenance. It is also an ideal moment to savour, not just the physical nourishment, but the nourishment we gain from breaking bread with those significant others in our lives.

You may feel uncomfortable when you introduce a new ceremony into your life, and you may meet resistance from other family members, but if your intention is clear and you do it with meaning and integrity then it will become easier.

We don't feel in the least awkward when decorating our homes at Christmas, for example, so take heart.

Another way to introduce ceremony and ritual into the house is to set aside a place to have a house altar. This can be a tiny shelf somewhere, or a huge table. The size of the space doesn't matter.

My house altar is on the landing window ledge. To make my altar, I firstly thoroughly cleaned the space, before lighting a candle and dedicating it.

Here I have a small posy of flowers or berries, angel cards, crystals, inspirational sayings, a small statue and a candle.

Each morning as I go down the stairs I stop to greet the new day.

I light the candle, asking for blessings for the house and all beings that dwell in and around it, and I pick an angel card to reflect on.

I leave the candle alight (it is safely contained) until I go back upstairs, and then I think of people who would benefit from the light before blowing it out.

This only takes a very little time, but is a ritual which is very meaningful to me and creates a Pause Point when I am fully present in the moment and not in mid-dash to do something else.

I also use the window ledge in the hall as a nature table. Do you remember this from your schooldays? We were encouraged to be outside and to keep our eyes open for interesting seed heads, conkers, acorns, animal skulls, etc. Well, I have revisited this idea and find that it is something else which acts as a focus for observing seasonal changes. As I write this it is late Autumn and I have collected a few conkers, seed heads of wild clematis or old man's beard, and the most beautiful acorn cups, which remind me of fairy drinking goblets.

An old pottery vase is filled with feathers, and after a visit to a local pumpkin farm I now have an arrangement of the most photogenic gourds that are just begging to be painted as a still life. It has sharpened my eye, and as the seasons progress so I will change the display. It has surprised me how much I have enjoyed doing it and how beautiful it looks in the house.

I also have large, crazy pictures hanging on my walls that have been made from beach finds. I have burnt messages into driftwood, added shells, twine, bird feathers, and hung pebbles threaded with coloured wool.

The sea can teach us about cycles, ebbs and flows, and change.

I find that having objects from the natural world around me anchors me to the landscape into which my body will eventually return to, and that makes me feel quite happy.

I F AN elderly relative or a person with a terminal illness wants to talk about their death or their funeral arrangements, try to allow them to do so. Please don't change the subject because you do not know how to handle it. Be brave and have the conversation.

It is one of the kindest things you will ever do, and is honouring them in a very special way. Not talking about their death will not keep them here.

Don't worry if you get upset or don't know what to say. Listen to what they want to talk about and answer them from the heart.

"I organized my father's funeral with my siblings. It was an honour to say goodbye in the best way we could. He and I had talked about the hymns he would like before he died. This was a very special time."

MY MOTHER shopped for a beautiful lawn nightdress for her funeral as carefully as if she was going to a party, and in a way she was.

R EFLECT ON the following. If this feels like too much then come back to it. But try to ponder on it a little and you just might need to do a little homework before you can answer it anyway.

• What sort of coffin do you want to be buried in? There is a huge choice! Will an oak one with brass handles reflect who you are? Or would you better suit a wicker casket or a bamboo one? A cardboard coffin sounds horrid, but is not at all as they come in different colours and can look much softer than wood.

It is also quite possible to decorate and paint cardboard coffins to really reflect and celebrate the life of the person who has died.

I think they're lovely for a child's coffin as the whole family can be involved in drawing on it and in its decoration.

I recently looked at wicker coffins and was told by

the funeral director that until it was needed, it actually made a rather practical storage unit, and if upended, and with the addition of a couple of shelves, would double as a rather trendy bookcase!

A friend has bought one because she feels she needs to be familiar and comfortable with it.

She says very matter of factly, that "she knows she's going to wear it one day". For the time being it houses her sewing equipment until eventually it will house her.

- Make sure you write down how looking at this made you feel.

It would be really helpful if there is a friend you can chat with about today's task. "You'll NEVER guess what I've been asked to look at today!"

LET'S LOOK at how you feel about aging. We are put under a lot of peer and media pressure to not show signs of aging. We live in such an ageist society.

> *"I feel I have lost my youth and sometimes my vitality just through natural aging. The next ten years are crucial to enjoy. I don't cope well with loss but I am sure I will enjoy what's left as long as I can walk. I have a huge amount of hope but sometimes I get frantic with all the things I want to do and so little time...."*

- What steps do you take to appear more youthful? Why is this? Really take the time to explore your thoughts.

- Have you been made redundant or feel as though your life is of no value? Or that you don't fit in? Take a while to reflect on this.

- Find photos of Native American elders and look at the wisdom in their faces. Look at how comfortable they make us feel.

Begin to ask yourself questions like why, for example, you keep dying your hair.

Are you really happy with still doing it? If you are, then that is absolutely fine. But if you would quite like to stop then why not do so?

Honour your grey hairs, your lines, your changing body shape. They are all signs that you have journeyed far in this lifetime, that you have lived, that you have gained wisdom and knowledge.

Begin to look for this wisdom in others who are further along the life path than you, and realize the value and the contribution to society they still can make.

- In your notebook make a list of ten people who have, in their lifetime, made a contribution to society during their "wisdom" years.

The list may include your Granny, whose weekly visits to the local primary school to hear readers is looked forward to by many of the children as a chance to be nurtured. She may also run the after-school knitting club. Or possibly your octogenarian, vegetable-growing neighbour who is your gardening guru? How about Mother Teresa who continued her work into her eighties? Or Sir David Attenborough for still managing to inspire us with his wisdom and insights into the natural world?

- Is there someone of more advanced years than yourself with whom you can strike up a mutually nurturing relationship?

L ESSONS ABOUT death can be found in the most unexpected places. I settled down to watch the children's film 'Mr Magorium's Wonder Emporium', and ended up with a life lesson that has stayed with me. Mr Magorium owns a magical toyshop, helped by three misfits: Molly Mahoney, a frustrated pianist, Henry Weston, an oddball child, and Eric Applebaum, who is called in to help but lives for his work. Mr Magorium is 243 years old, and had bought enough shoes to last him his lifetime. His last pair has holes in the soles and he knows that it is approaching the time for him to depart.

He is very straightforward and fearless about this but just wants to leave the Emporium in good hands. Molly refuses at first to accept that he is serious about his death and tries to talk him out of it. She prepares a day of simple delights for him, such as dancing on giant bubble wrap in the park. However Mr Magorium refuses to focus on anything except the joy in the moment. The film is profoundly inspiring, thought-provoking and suggests we must believe in the magic in our lives right now.

I keep having Mr Magorium moments when I actively feel delight in some small task or activity I am engaged in. If one can have a fictitious mentor then Mr Magorium is mine.

"Millions long for immortality who don't know what to do with themselves on a rainy Sunday afternoon."

Susan Ertz

- Who is an inspirational teacher or mentor for you?

WHY IS it such a dilemma about whether or not children should go to funerals? Why not ask them if they want to go, having explained what takes place. Or are we too afraid of displaying emotions in front of them, or appearing out of control? It does, of course, need sensitive handling.

It may be very moving when a young child reads a lesson, poem or similar at a parent's funeral but it needs to be carefully gauged as to whether it is appropriate and why the child has been asked. Will it be in the child's best interests?

• What are your thoughts on this?

A FRIEND wanted her husband's ashes put into a carrier bag, rather than in an urn, and was planning to scatter them over her rose bed. Never having looked at ashes before, she was worried that there may be visible bits of bone left. She discussed her thoughts openly, which I found refreshing and actually very amusing.

We all have our own ways of dealing with the ashes, and all are perfectly okay. Many of us would find it hard to be so matter of fact about them, but equally, people are coming up with novel ways of disposing of ashes, even scattering them into space in a firework display.

Another possibility is to have your loved one's ashes made into a diamond and set into an item of jewellery. There are various companies who offer this unique service.

HAVE YOU decided yet whether you want to be buried or cremated? If the former, do you want to be interred in a graveyard, in a natural burial site or even at home?

There are many possibilities as long as legal requirements are met.

The 'New Natural Death Handbook' has guidelines, although each local authority may have different rules.

Natural burial sites are on the increase as demand grows for real alternatives to a church-based graveyard or being cremated.

It may surprise you but being cremated isn't as green a choice as you would think.

A natural burial site is normally run as a wildlife sanctuary. The graves are unmarked by headstones, although all are micro-chipped and recorded on a site plan.

People can choose to plant a native tree and many sites encourage nesting boxes. Our local centre is fabulous, full of wild flowers and brimming with wildlife.

People are invited to spend time there, walking, sitting and watching. Coffins are taken down to their plots on an old-fashioned handcart.

My friend was buried there in winter and her wicker coffin had been decorated with ivy and other evergreen hedgerow plants. As she was a child of nature it was entirely appropriate and it felt like a true celebration and an honouring of whom she was.

PLEASE MOURN properly for your animals. Take time off work, cry, bury them well. To many people an animal is as precious to them as a child, and yet society expects them to just get over their death. Well don't! Grieve well. It is not a crime. If people do not understand then find someone who does. There are plenty of us out there. A bereavement helpline is in the Resources on page 102.

When I lost my beloved cat I needed to grieve for her loss in no less a way than when my Mother died, whom I also loved dearly. It was just as sad.

Why would we not mourn for a companion who has showered us with unconditional love for so many years?

When I lose any animal I have an appropriate ceremony. I like to dig their graves myself, lining them with soft fabric, straw, or even rosemary (for remembrance). I often put a crystal in with them and sprinkle rose petals on their still forms, before covering them. I always mark their graves with whatever seems appropriate.

Sometimes I will mark it with a small sculpture, sometimes with a plant.

Bereaved clients often comment on how guilty they feel because they actually feel more heartbroken over the loss of their pet than they did when a relative died. I put this down to the extra close bond we can share with an animal, which is often difficult with a human.

Our animals rarely make us feel the negative emotions that we can experience when entering into a relationship with a human.

Think about it. When did an animal ever make you feel jealous or unloved, angry or rejected? When did an animal ever criticize you?

Animals can be our soul mates and we can feel really heartbroken when we lose them.

"I lost my wonderful dog after a year of care. He was a fantastic trooper who enjoyed life to the end. I was absolutely devastated. Most people understood and dreaded the day as they knew he was my little boy. Sadly there is no allowance at

work under the special leave categories for grieving for a pet."

- Have you lost a pet? Did you mark their death? If you didn't and you regret not having done so then it is never too late to do so in a way which seems appropriate to you.

*****

"Saul was a traveller. He lived in a caravan, reared pigs and had these wonderful Shire horses. He took me under his wing and taught me how to drive my Shire cross horse. He had a fantastic two-horse set up and we both went to a heavy horse show, me with my old refurbished scotch tip cart and he with his fantastic set dripping the shiniest brass you could imagine.

He dropped dead at that show, all 6' 4" of him, just down like a tree."

Saul died with absolutely no warning. If we were all

to go like this in what ways do you think it would change how we live?

Is it better to go like Saul, immersed in doing what he loved? Or would you prefer a diagnosis and a predicted time scale?

Since hearing about Saul it has made me more diligent about keeping my affairs in order.

• Have you known someone who was here one minute and dead the next? How did it affect you and those around you? What emotions did you experience? Did you change the way you live? Have you kept up the changes or have they become less significant?

I HAD an interesting discussion with a girlfriend today about someone she knew who had just a few months to live. She was given the option to have an operation followed by chemotherapy but this would only give her a month or two longer. This woman opted instead to leave her children and go and spend four of her remaining five months with a healer in Brazil who helped a great number of cancer patients. This she did, and my friend reported that although she died a month after her return, she had had a fantastic time and had returned looking well and calm.

My friend found it hard to believe that she had not wanted to spend every second of those last few months with her children. I found it amazing that this woman had the courage to follow her truth, to spend her time as she thought best, in preparing herself for death. I believe that the time spent with the healer was valuable "soul medicine", and that if she died in a place of calm then it would have taught her children a great deal.

But it did raise a question for me. If I knew I had

only so much time left then how would I spend it? What about you?

I guess, in truth, we can only know the answer if it becomes our reality.

- Have you known people in this situation? What is their story?

WHEN MY Mother died it seemed to take an age for it to happen. She would take a long shuddering breath and then nothing. Then suddenly her chest would heave and she would take another breath. What I remember most about her death are her feet. She had a hole in her sock and her big toe was peeping through. It was so human.

Soup

As the blade slices through the onion's pungency
I see my Mother's hands, long burnt
in the furnace flames, deftly slicing
and chopping for the soup pot.
I have peeled a layer of my memory
and it stings as I recall
she had a hole in her sock
the day she died
and her toe nail needed cutting.
I had put my finger in the hole
to stop her soul from leaving,
but it must have slithered past
at the other end
as she never breathed again.
It was the last part of her I ever touched,
it was her last stock pot
and now I just stir up memories.

Sally Petch

I ALWAYS feel it is an honour to be with someone when they pass, but if that fills you with dread then do not do it. Do not be there. That's fine too. If you do get to be there then try not to hold them here. Tell them, either silently or aloud, that it's okay for them to go.

At these times I have found it very helpful to softly repeat the beautiful and powerful prayer of St. Julian of Norwich:

"All shall be well,
And all shall be well,
And all manner of things shall be well."

It is helpful if we can learn to "hold a space" for the dying, to not let our emotions crowd the space. There will be another time for that.

The more a person is relaxed with the advent of death, the easier it seems to be to cross.

"I have a vision that it's a little like leaving a house
before going on holiday. One wants to make sure it

is shut down properly, that notes have been left, that everything is clean, tidy and in its place; things are switched off at the mains, the lights are off, one final look around to check and then out, closing the door quietly behind you and on into freedom and new adventures."

*****

"My Mother told us she was going to die. She said goodbye to us in her own way. A short time later as she lay peacefully in bed growing weaker and weaker she would lift her hand slowly and wave at me from time to time until finally she took a deep breath and was gone. I always had a sense that she participated fully in her own passing, which my sister and I were privileged to witness."

What a gift this woman gave to her children. Her last act of love on the earthly plane. It seemed that she was fully participating in this part of her journey. This can be practised in our daily living.

- Right at this moment be fully present. That means putting down the book, and being aware of your body, how you're feeling, the sounds around you, the people around you, and just being in that space.

I T IS often said that men can only do one thing at once whilst women can easily multitask. It is praised as an asset, as something to be proud of, but I ask you, is it an asset? If we are talking on the phone, whilst picking up the children from school, nipping into the shops on the way home to grab a ready meal, whilst trying to remember where we've put the novel we're meant to be discussing at book group that evening, how rooted in the moment can we be? Did we get comfortable in the car, concentrating only on driving safely and sending out blessings to other drivers? I suspect not.

Did we have time to pull into the layby to better watch the kestrel hovering overhead or to see if we can see the end of the rainbow that has manifested ahead of us? I suspect not. Did we even notice the journey other than something to be endured? Is this a parable of our lives? There are times when I wonder how women actually have the time to die!

WHEN MY sister was dying she suddenly became very animated, and although she was unable to speak, she managed to convey to me that she could see Mum and Gran at the bottom of her bed. She was so excited and overjoyed. It gave me great comfort to know that they were waiting for her.

- There are numerous stories of the dying seeing friends or relatives as they are part way between this world and the next. What are your thoughts on this?

THERE SEEMS to be a consensus amongst people who have shared the moment of death with someone in that there is a definite change in the feeling around the body.

Nurses can sense this and some have become very attuned to knowing when it is appropriate to move the body. Other people are skilled at helping a person's soul to fully leave the earth plane and move on to where they should be.

"I worked with a Trinidadian computer programmer who was involved in a road accident and was taken to hospital where I visited him.

He was in intensive care, unconscious and attached to breathing apparatus and with wires and tubes all over him. He was naked to the waist but had no visible signs of injury. I went in to see him for more than a week and I used to pray as I stood by him and hold a one-sided conversation with him. Once I held his hand. Some days later his family arrived from Trinidad. One day I went to visit. There were no staff around and he looked the same with all his equipment and the pump rhythmically going up and down. But as soon as I went into the room and looked at him I sensed that he was dead.

I approached him and he looked just the same but I just knew he was no longer there.

Then a nurse appeared and told me he was brain dead and they were about to switch off the life support machine. The essential "He" had gone and although I felt sadness at the loss of a young life I had a sense that all was not lost and that he had passed on to the next world."

It has been widely noted that there is a point at which people can identify that the energy has changed around someone who has died.

- Have you experienced this? Did you find it reassuring?

"I was in the hospital when my brother's partner, who was my close friend, died. In the afternoon I sat and gave her healing and I saw her lying out of her body above the bed. In the evening I again gave her healing and this time she was standing up with her arms raised. I knew it would not be long and asked the angels why she could not be released. I was told there was a time to be born and a time to die. She left her body two hours later. It was a very beautiful experience, although her breathing was difficult towards the end, but I knew she was out of her body and ready to leave."

NEXT TIME you are in a stationery store buy a scrapbook or a folder. Make sure it is sturdy and a pleasure to get out and use. This will be your death book. In this you will slip everything to do with your own death.

I chose a purple photo album decorated with flowers. Make sure that people know where it is as it will contain all the information they will need when you die. And yes, they will not want to hear this and they may even laugh at you, but tell them anyway.

Update it when people are around so that it becomes familiar to them.

What do you insert? Make sure you enclose any banking details with the passwords or numbers. Put this in an unmarked sealed envelope.

Include your will, insurance documents, etc. And then the interesting ongoing stuff. The song on a CD that you would like played at your funeral, the poem you connected with when you heard it last summer. Anything to do with planning this one last great celebration. The bit I love is how much I change this as *I* change. What spoke to me last year may not this year, but as the whole album is in pencil, and the poems are tucked in on separate sheets of paper, I just remove things and update.

And do you know I really enjoy doing it, as the process helps me to get to know myself and clarify who I am. And for people to know who you are at your funeral is a parting gift *you* can give *them*.

I have been to funerals where the readings have been so insightful, that I have felt that even after their death, I have learnt something new about the deceased.

Also in this album are photos of some of my possessions and written on the back of the photo are the details of whom I would like it to be given to, along with their contact details.

Make sure these are kept updated too, or if you let go of that item that you remove the photo. It's surprising how often I have had to do this because I have given the object to the person already.

Friends who know about my death book are now very wary of coming into my house and admiring anything, without a degree of sincerity, as there is a chance it will end up on their mantelpiece!

Any item I pass on goes with the instruction that if the recipient tires of it, they are to pass it on to someone else who would benefit from it.

I just do not hold with keeping an ornament just because it was given to you, either as a birthday or Christmas present or as a bequest. I strongly believe that you should only have the things around you which are of real use, or which you love.

Anything else I pass on to someone who does appreciate it. There's no accounting for taste!

*****

"I did not want to see my father after he had died, but forced myself to. I was so glad I did because he really wasn't in that body any more and it took away my fears about him being buried."

Again there are no rights and wrongs here. I did not want to see my Mother, but agreed to accompany my Father. He thought she looked wonderful.

I thought she looked unlike my Mother. They had done her hair in a style she never would have worn, and had set her face. She also smelt odd; not unpleasant, just not her.

I would have preferred my last sight of her to have been in the hospital bed with her hair awry and her jaw all twisted. It was more honest. I did not need her to be tidied up and sanitized.

- Have you ever seen a dead person? Write about it in your journal and how it made you feel.

ARE YOU afraid of dying or the dying process? If you are, what exactly is it you are afraid of? Is it the unknown? Is it leaving loved ones? Is it a fear of family and friends seeing you suffering? Spend time just thinking about this. You may find it difficult, but understanding what the fear is about will help you begin to overcome it.

Think about opening up a dialogue about this with a friend or partner. Maybe they will be glad to voice their fears too.

Be open to reading about near-death experiences. They can be a comfort.

JUST IMAGINE you knew you were going to die today. Stay with that thought for a moment. How would you spend those hours? Will you write the letter of complaint to the manager of your local store because they overcharged you on one item or will you contact all your loved ones and share the time with them?

Or spend time outside feeling the sun on your face and listening to the bird song or fussing your pet? I suspect the letter of complaint will not be high on the agenda.

Why not go outside right now and really look at something of beauty? And then ring your best friend just to tell them you loved their new outfit and thought they looked fabulous in it. Is there anyone you have said unkind things to? Well, maybe now is the time to open up a dialogue with them again.

Make sure you spend time telling your loved ones how much they mean to you. Do not let an opportunity pass to tell them you love them.

I F WE think about dying when we are well, the fears can be worse than when we are approaching death. Have you noticed with elderly people how their lives begin to close in? Many want to stay within their home environment, and gradually lose interest in hobbies. This is just part of the shutting down process; the being comfortable of what is coming next. After all, none of us really like to leave unfinished business, so when we are making our final exit it is good to be mentally ready.

HAVE YOU ever been with a terminally ill person? There often comes a point when they seem to accept that their death is imminent. They turn inward, some seem to do a lot of mental preparation, and often seem to be content to slip away.

It is the people they leave behind who have the hard time of it.

Many times I have counselled clients who have been distraught because the person they had lost chose to die at the very moment that they had taken a break from the bedside to grab a coffee.

They are racked with guilt that they were not there at the end.

Notice I wrote "chose to die". It is sometimes easier for a person to die when they are on their own.

The strength of our love can sometimes hold them here past their time. So it is no coincidence that when you had nipped out for a moment they slipped away. Do not feel bad about it. It was meant to happen like that. In the same way that someone can hang on, seemingly defying death, until a loved one has arrived at their bedside.

> *"I was with my Father when he died. He had been in bed for some time due to the lack of physical strength in old age, although his mind was still clear. After breakfast – which he'd eaten with relish – he mentioned a bit of pain between his shoulder blades. I rubbed it for him and suggested getting a doctor if it didn't improve. "That won't be necessary chicken" (his pet name for us), he said. Laying him back comfortably on the pillows I went to the kitchen, whereupon I felt something very strongly. I threw down the tray and ran back to his room. He was laying back, eyes closed, but I knew he was dying. I got up on the bed beside him and whispered his favourite prayer, imploring him to wait until Mam got there, which he did before dying in her arms."*

There are as many ways to choose to die as there are to live. All are fine.

"I've told my children that when I die, to release balloons in the sky to celebrate that I graduated. For me death is a graduation."

Elizabeth Kubler-Ross

I WANT to talk now about treating illness. Never lose sight of the fact that it is your body and that you can have as many treatments as you feel you want or you can have none. The choice really is yours. So many of us give our power away to a member of the medical profession, and quite frankly some of us are kept alive because we do not have the strength to fight doctors or our loved ones. Do you really want that course of chemotherapy? Will you do anything to avoid dying?

If you are not ill at this very moment and your answer is yes, then you need to begin to explore your fear of death.

WORKING WITH Flower Essences can be really powerful during times of death or other life transitions. When used with the terminally ill they can prepare the soul for departure, and they can be invaluable for the bereaved.

Don't forget your animals. They too can go through a grieving process if their companion, either human or animal, departs.

Flower Essences work just as well with them. Try Bach Flower Sweet Chestnut for extreme anguish, and Bach Flower Walnut for any time of transition.

When my sister was dying we used Walnut a lot with her to help her adjust to changes at a soul level.

People who have to live with a loved one who has suffered a stroke can also go through a bereavement process, as the person they once knew has changed.

Again Flower Essences are helpful. They are safe to take and can be self-diagnosed.

If you would prefer to visit a Flower Essence practitioner, who will combine Essences for you and adapt it when necessary, then contact the British Flower and Vibrational Essences Association (see Resources on page 102).

IT IS so important to celebrate and mark times of transition in our lives. If we have gone through a really trying time then we should mark the passing of it in some positive way. These challenging times make us stronger and teach us valuable life lessons that we are here to learn. If you have just gone through a divorce or been made redundant then seek to have a proper closure. Have a divorce party with your closest girlfriends. Or at the very least go out for afternoon tea and eat cake! It is so important that we not let these occasions just pass by.

Do not leave it up to your partner, family or friends to organize something as they probably will not think it appropriate to do so. But it is.

If you have been made redundant then praise yourself for all the years of service you gave. It does not matter if it was a stressful time. You owe it to yourself to say, "Hey, I did well". If finances allow, buy yourself a luxury to mark the closure. It can even be something for the garden. How about purchasing the rose, 'Peace'? And then organising a planting ceremony?

Be very clear about why you are planting it: to celebrate closure and new beginnings. Invite a friend along and have a glass of champagne or sparkling wine as you water in the plant.

"I got divorced and the day was memorable because as I came out of the court building the heavens just opened in a huge cloudburst. It felt as though all my cares had just washed away and I never looked back again."

*****

"I lost my job on my birthday, and it was the best birthday ever. I recognize my reaction is not common, but what helped me was my utter joy at being free to do whatever I wanted. I founded the Oyster Club, for people like me, for whom the world is their oyster. Something had happened that many would regard as devastating but the upside is the freedom it suddenly bestows."

IF YOU have lost a dear soul, have had the funeral, but it still doesn't feel as though you've done enough to honour them then it may help to plant a memory garden. It need only be a small patch of ground, but could include a couple of their favourite plants, or flowers in a range of their favourite colours. Maybe a statue? Or a bench? Did they love wildlife? Then how about including a bird feeder or a nesting box?

There will also be times when we are very fond of someone who has died but who is not deemed to be particularly close to us by the relatives. What comes to my mind are the clients of mine who have died. I may get an invite to the funeral but that is often the only opportunity I will have to mark their passing, so in that case I will go and buy a plant and add it to my own memory garden.

Let your imagination take over. Imagine they are there helping you to design it, and it will soon take shape. It will help you to feel connected to them, will give you a purpose, and will expose you to the healing power of nature.

Put in a bench and think how lovely it would be to sit in that part of your garden in the summer, surrounded by memories of the people you have cared about.

HAVE YOU ever lost a physical part of you? It could be anything that was once part of your body, from a kidney to a leg, a breast to a tooth. It is so important to mourn that loss. I think we underrate the spiritual significance of surgery. Our aura, the invisible energy that surrounds our body like a second layer, still surrounds the missing part.

This is why, when people have an amputation, they can still "feel" and have pain in that area. If you are going to have surgery why not have a ceremony beforehand, and bless and thank the part of your body that is going to be operated on.

We mind so much about losing objects. Why do we not care more when we lose an actual part of us?

Healing will be a lot quicker if you have done some acceptance work beforehand.

Talk about your impending loss to a close friend or partner. You may want to mix up an aromatherapy oil and anoint that part or area. It may be significant to light a candle and place a photo of yourself before it. But treat this part with a lot of love. Tell it you will miss it and thank it for all the service it has done you.

A WOMAN'S womb is her seat of creativity, both in a physical and a spiritual sense. If you are having, or have had, a hysterectomy it is important that you pursue creative activities that you find stimulating and nurturing, and which regularly lead to a manifestation of your work on the physical plane. Take up watercolor painting, garden design, cushion making or writing. This is equally as important if you are going, through, or have gone through, the menopause. Again this is a transition, and it needs to be marked.

WHEN WE have had surgery our "outer layers" may have been damaged. If a wound is slow to heal we may need to have work done on that part of our aura in order to heal the hidden wounds. The Alaskan Gem Essence Rhodolite Garnet will assist in healing of this nature.

When the body has undergone this sort of trauma and loss it is so important to treat it for shock. All of the Flower Essence ranges do a "rescue remedy" for just this occasion. Bach Flower Rescue Remedy is the most universally known.

Take this for some days before surgery, immediately before you go to theatre, as soon after as you are able, and then continue for a few days.

If someone is going to be with you right after surgery, or you are unconscious, then the remedy can be applied to pulse points or put onto a helper's hands and smoothed down the whole body, keeping the hands just above. This sinks the rescue remedy into the aura. This can also be done if someone has an accident and is unconscious. Apply to pulse points or put onto your hands and just skim above the body. Trust me, it works.

I have done this on wild birds, hens and cats. It has an immediate and perceptible calming effect.

And if the person dies it will ease their crossing. Remember it is not appropriate to save everyone. People in our care ARE going to die. It is what people do!

HAVE YOU had an abortion, lost a baby during pregnancy, had a stillbirth? Maybe you mourned for this soul? Maybe not? If this is pertinent to you, then just take a moment now to reflect on how comfortable you feel with your thoughts. Is there any work you still need to do? Do you need to start grieving for that aborted soul even though it may be years later? This is not about beating yourself up. It is about acknowledging a loss. That is it. No more.

That soul came through for that short time to be with you for a reason. It would have been aware its time was limited and that is perfectly okay.

How did your life change as a result of your loss? What did you learn? If you are not sure then re-examine it. If it brings up emotions then let them come out.

Do not suppress them again. Really grieve for that little soul and thank them for being a part of your life.

And remember that they chose to fulfil that role in your life so just let go of the guilt right now! It is inappropriate to feel guilt and it devalues their gift to you. All is just as it should be. All is well.

ARE YOU the father of a child who has been lost to you? Either because you had no rights over an abortion issue or you may be the father of a stillborn baby. Make sure you are gentle with yourself and that you mourn for the loss. All too often peoples' messages of sympathy and offers of help can seem to be directed at the mother because she has had the physical trauma.

However, you have shared in the emotional trauma and deserve to be treated with just as much compassion. So take time off work, rest and recover.

"I still haven't properly had my closure on the abortion. I have bought a Chinese lantern, which I hope my girlfriend and I may set off together on the anniversary of the termination. I had thought of getting a tattoo to mark that part of my life as it was important to us both."

WHAT DO you believe happens to you when you die? What are your beliefs about an afterlife? About reincarnation, about heaven, hell, karma, nirvana? It is really important to begin to form ideas, even if it is that when you die, that is it. Blackness.

I have spent a lifetime working on my spiritual beliefs and have been blessed with many affirmations as to what happens to us on a soul level when we die. It is my understanding that we can experience many lifetimes on Earth where we learn, change, and help others on their path, either mindfully or unmindfully. I believe our aim is to try to remain in a place of connection and love despite our own personal challenges.

We are all here for a purpose, and the more you work with that in mind the clearer yours may become. Sometimes our purpose may be one of sacrifice, of teaching, healing or inspirational work in the arts. But even if we feel we have not made a great contribution we have all touched people in a myriad of unknown ways.

There have been occasions when I have caught up with a pupil I had taught when I was in primary education or a former client and they will often remark on something I had said to them that they remember to this day and that influenced them at the time.

I would have been totally unaware of this and it makes me feel a small frisson of anxiety about possible negative things I have said that may have done the same. I can only endeavour to be more mindful in every moment.

I BELIEVE too that we can be in contact with those who have crossed before us if we choose to be. I have been to excellent mediums who have given me messages, which I know to be true.

I have also seen and felt my mother after she died. I would like to say it was comforting, but it actually scared me half to death! However, she relayed something to me of great significance.

When I later visited a medium, one of her first sentences was to tell me that my mother apologised for frightening me so much, and promised she would not come through like that again. She has been true to her word but there are many ways she still lets me know that she is around.

These are a few snapshots of some of *my* beliefs. They have allowed me to be completely comfortable with the idea of my own death.

Your beliefs may be completely different to mine, and that is absolutely fine. What is not fine is if you have not begun to form any sort of belief system, or have simply refused to look at it because it means you have to think of death.

Begin to read, to ask people, to listen to other people's ideas. Be open minded. See how you resonate with them. Go to a church service, visit a temple, talk to a rabbi.

Begin, if you have not already, to explore this fascinating subject. Something will strike a cord with you and will feel "true". And as you begin to feel comfortable around death so you will begin to live your life without the fear of dying. And that is indeed a liberating feeling.

IMAGINE IF you were to die today. Imagine your nearest and dearest opening your dressing table drawers or your wardrobe. Does the thought horrify you? If it does, then do something about it. Cupboard by cupboard, file by file, start to get it all in order. This will have the most amazingly positive benefits in your life. It will free up energy and will make you feel in control. You will know where things are, and if you are discarding lots of stuff then other people and charity shops will benefit too. I always find that when I'm clutter clearing that it helps to consider a charity close to my heart.

If you have a lot of possessions and a lot of unsorted unorganized paperwork then do not despair. The rule is to sort and sift little and often. Do one drawer a day or one handful of paper a day. Stop long before you are bored or tired. Every time you do it it will get easier. In fact it can even become addictive. Another way to start is to make it feel playful. Get a kitchen timer and set it for 15 minutes and then race against the clock. Can you tidy your whole sock drawer in that time? Give it a go. When the pinger goes then reward yourself with a cup of tea and a biscuit!

HAVE YOU made your will yet? If you haven't, then why not look up a solicitor, if you don't have one already? How about picking up the phone and making an appointment? Or there are many will-writing services to be found on the internet. If your will is not complicated then it need only take an hour to do. Some banks offer their account holders a free will-writing service and charities such as the Wildfowl and Wetland Trusts offer a free will-writing month from time to time.

I have just finalized mine and I can honestly say that it felt really satisfying to have it done and settled.

Many people feel that they may be tempting fate to instigate a will and they defer it until the time is right, whenever that may be. We never know our departure date and for some of us it could be sooner rather than later, and we may not have the luxury of time.

This following poem (taken from 'Watching for the Kingfisher' by Ann Levin) brings this sharply into focus.

DEATH MATTERS

Year's Mind

Every year, I pass the day
Not knowing. Someday
Someone will say, "Oh yes,
Ann died a year ago".

Makes you think, doesn't it?

I HAVE a client who does not want a funeral service. She wants to leave her wicker coffin on display and wants people to pop in and pin a farewell message to it. She will then go with these wishes and they will be burnt with her.

• How do you feel about this idea? Sometimes when we find a thought unpleasant it can teach us a great deal because it puts us more in touch with what we feel, for us, is appropriate and comfortable.

WHAT COLOUR do you want people to wear at your funeral? It may be that you think black is the only appropriate shade to wear.

I want people to wear bright colours to mine. I loathe black and dislike having to wear it to funerals. It makes me feel even more depressed. Colour has a marked effect on our aura, our well-being and our emotions.

A friend recently went to a funeral where everyone had to wear pink. The men were allowed either shirts or ties; they did not have to go out and purchase a Liberace number! She said it was great.

Pink is the colour of the heart, of our emotions and of love. What a perfect colour to wear to the funeral of someone we love. Again it is all about our own preferences, but it is important to have them!

When I discussed this with a friend she said she always wore black to funerals because it reflected her sombre mood. She would dislike it if people turned up in anything else to her funeral. So it is important to write your preference clearly into your death book.

A FRIEND can not come to terms with the idea of her children seeing her dying. It is a real fear. She is quite well at the moment but we are looking at this inevitable issue, and coming up with some possible solutions. It does not help to tell her she may die suddenly, perhaps of a heart attack, when her children are nowhere around.

We all have our fears around the subject of death. Some of us fear dying alone, some in an undignified manner. I have asked my spirit guides that I be allowed to die in bed with my beloved animals around me and I do hold on to that as a focus. I find it helps.

- How would you like to die?

IT WOULD have been my Mother's 90th birthday this week. We celebrated it by going to an outdoor theatre performance. She would have loved this. Funny that it coincided with her actual birthday. Even stranger, that my partner found some money on the pavement the day after we had booked the tickets! There were several times when I felt her presence there that evening.

- When you have lost a loved one, have you ever smelt a perfume in the room, or cigar smoke, for example? Or seen a movement out of the corner of your eye?

Or the person has come into your mind so clearly, or you thought you heard their voice? But how could you? They are dead. Well, yes actually you can. Just cancel out the critical, logical side of you and let the intuitive side have free rein for a while.

Why not try talking to the person as though they were still physically in the room with you? People seem to find this easier to do at gravesides but I just do it when I need to, or when I sense that for some reason a deceased person has tried to make contact.

We always have to explain things to fit in with our world view. If it does not then we dismiss it as fanciful. In the words of Shakespeare's Hamlet: *"There are more things in heaven and earth, Horatio, than are dreamt of in your philosophy"*. I could not put that better myself!

A FRIEND had agreed a prearranged sign with her dying friend so that she would know she was okay after she'd passed. It is something many people try to arrange and yet it doesn't seem to work out. I have no doubt that the dead do try to communicate with us but not in a way that has been prearranged. And because you are so busy looking out for that one message, it blinds you to the very real messages that the deceased is trying to get you to understand!

- Have you had any experiences of this?

DO YOU have any favourite poems or readings you are considering putting into your death book yet?

When I asked this question of a large number of people, W. H. Auden's 'Funeral Blues' seemed to tug at the heartstrings. This was the poem used in the film 'Four Weddings and a Funeral'. I think it's a beautiful thought that someone might choose to read it at a funeral but it isn't in my death book funeral wishes as it is just so full of heartache and despair.

Other popular choices were 'Do Not Stand At My Grave And Weep' and 'Miss Me But Let Me Go'.

• Look up a poem and read it ALOUD. See how it triggers your emotions.

There are many websites dedicated to providing suitable poems. The problem is often that there really is not a lot of time to search for exactly the right poems and readings to make a memorable funeral and bereaved relatives are not in the right space to make snap decisions.

So any research you do now will help your loved ones, and you do only get one chance.

I would also hazard a guess that as you begin to read through the poems that they will bring to the surface lots of emotional stuff. And that can only be good.

A FUNERAL is rather like baking a cake. You need good preparation, the right quantity of ingredients and careful mixing to ensure success.

"When I had to organize my Mother's funeral it was very liberating because she died away from her home town and none of her elderly friends came. I felt this allowed us to do something true to her inner spirit. This obviously raised questions about whether those largely secular minded friends who knew her from bridge club would have felt it reflected my Mother's outer life. Probably they wouldn't. We later had a memorial service back where she had lived.

Overall I felt the two ceremonies and events associated with them pretty well summed up my Mother's internal diversions – the memorial service reflected her outer life, the funeral the radiant soul energy I often saw/felt in her."

*****

"A few years ago we went to two funerals in quite a short time, and there was a huge difference between them. The first was truly memorable and was for the mother of a friend. I thought I knew her quite well but the service was amazing. In the church the sun was streaming through the windows, there were flowers, smiles and the normally obligatory black was conspicuous by its absence.

The service was fantastic because of the eulogies and the feeling of love and friendliness. This little old lady had led the most amazing life and they really paid tribute to her. The second was in a crematorium, a similarly sunny day but there the similarity ended. It was a cold and unfeeling funeral as there was no personal tribute to the deceased at all, merely words from the service book."

"AM I going to die?" How often do we hear these words on TV while we are watching a medical drama? And we watch the anguished expressions on the face of the doctor, and the denial on the face of the relatives. There seems to be a moment of suspense before the medic hedges: "We don't know that. You must not give up hope". We all breathe again as we are not required to bear witness to a death, even if it is on our screens. There is a great disparity here with a crime drama where we often witness a murder. But this is done in such a way that we have become immune to these deaths, as they are a necessary part of the story, without which we wouldn't be able to solve the crime.

How much more refreshing would it be to say: "It seems likely, yes".

Because of course, nobody knows for sure when we will die. But die we will. It does not matter how much we rail against it. Die we will.

Honest words will allow the dying person to begin

to accept the inevitable. I would want to know. I do not want to give another person control by refusing to look at it. I have heard of families who have been informed of the likely outcome and have asked that the patient should not be told.

The overriding impression is that this is ending the relationship in a lie.

Goodbye

and did you know
that this
would be
your Deathday
you had not
been told
how ill.
you were not
involved
it was not
happening.
we were to
keep it
from you.
pretending
as always
and were you

DEATH MATTERS

keeping it
did you long
to cry out
I'm dying
yet say
nothing
you must have known

and did you
wonder
how we'd be
without you
and did you
feel afraid
and couldn't say
and did you
long to hold
to hold us
to you and say goodbye
goodbye

Pauline Prior-Pitt

Let's have it out in the open I say. Put it on the table. "There. In my professional opinion you will not live much longer."

You may want to spend your last days/weeks/ months on Earth searching for a cure or you may want to say okay, this is it. Let me prepare for it. Let me live this end by being authentic, by immersing myself in it, by feeling it, by trying to get just a little comfortable with it, by saying the things I need to say, and if I have the physical strength, to sort out my affairs.

"A dying man needs to die, as a sleepy man needs to sleep, and there comes a time when it is wrong, as well as useless, to resist."

Stewart Alsop

And if the fairy tale ending does shine on you? Then you will be a great deal less afraid of dying, you would have said things to people that you should have said anyway, and, my goodness, your paperwork and clothes cupboard will shine with common sense and clarity.

THE WORSE thing about my Sister's oncoming death was coping with Christmas Day. We all knew she only had days to go, weeks at the outside. She had wanted a "normal" Christmas. What on earth do you buy someone who is not going to be around longer than it takes to unwrap the gift? Of course I came up with things!

But in hindsight I probably would have given her gift boxes with words in them, like "I love you," or "I have loved having you as my sister". Words she could have kept with her as she began her withdrawal from the world. Oh yes, I can think of all sorts of meaningful things *now*.

But back then it was about getting through. For all of us. And let nobody tell you differently, it's hard.

But the soft wrap to have around her shoulders in bed, in the most beautiful colours imaginable, the pure essential oils with which to massage her hands, were appreciated and were eventually used elsewhere. Christmas was when I just wanted to yell, "Please don't go". I still weep as I write this as she died in her early fifties and we still had so much to do together.

However, we aren't born with a guarantee that we will last into old age. A lot of us don't, which makes it so vital that we are using our time on Earth in a way which is meaningful to us.

I do like the phrase "spending our time". I find it hugely powerful as it makes me think of our Earth time as a finite commodity.

So how do you want to spend yours? Doing a job you dislike but you only have a few years to go and jobs are hard to get in the current financial climate, on Facebook, watching reality TV, wandering around shops looking at goods you have no need of? If the answer to this is "yes", then that's fine as long as you are aware that the hour you have just spent trawling the internet will never be returned to you. It is spent. You can't earn it again.

It is too easy to spend our time in mediocrity. I heard a speaker recently talking about "doing work", "doing good work" or "doing great work", and I now have a memo on my desk which asks if I am doing "great work"?

I may not be, but I have my eye on the timer, and I am aware of the sand trickling, and that in each minute there is the potential to spend my time wisely and to take a step towards "great work".

- Write a list in your journal of all the things you would have liked to have tried in this lifetime if you'd been rich enough, young enough, thin enough, brave enough.

Now just see if there is one of those you can actually take one step towards achieving.

Remember *"It is never too late to be what you might have become"*. I love that. I have it written all over the place because until the fat lady sings it isn't too late.

I WANT to give the last page to a man I heard about last week, who had meticulously planned his own funeral.

It was the solemn moment when the curtains were closing around the coffin and the music began. What was it? The theme music from the film 'The Great Escape'.

Be quite sure he retreated to the sound of laughter. Humour followed him in death as it had in life and all there were blessed by it. A perfect ending.

I wish you good endings.

Acknowledgements

I would like to thank the following for permission to reproduce from their publications:

Hymns Ancient and Modern for the poem *Year's Mind* by Ann Lewin from 'Watching for the Kingfisher' (2009)

Goodbye from 'Waiting Women' by Pauline Prior-Pitt (1989)

Soup is by the author.

Resources

The Natural Death Centre
In The Hill House, Watley Lane, Tynford,
Winchester. SO21 1QX
Tel: +44 (0)1962 712690
www.naturaldeath.org.uk

International Flower Essences Repertoire
Achamore House, Isle of Gigha, Argyll,
Scotland. PA41 7AD
Tel: +44 (0)1583 505385
www.healingorchids.com

Bach Flowers
The Bach Centre, Mount Vernon, Bakers Lane,
Brightwell-cum-Sotwell, Oxon. OX10 0PZ
Tel;+ 44(0)1491 834678
www.bachcentre.com

The British Flower & Vibrational Essences Association
(BFVEA)
BM BFVEA, London WC1N 3XX
Tel; +44 (o)1308 458784
www.bfvea.com

Animal Samaritans Pet Bereavement Service:
Tel: 020 83031859
www.animalsamaritans.org.uk

'Sacred Celebrations: A Sourcebook' by Glennie
Kindred. (2001) ISBN 0 906362 48 2

'The New Natural Death Handbook' edited by Nicholas
Albery, Gil Elliot and Joseph Elliot (Natural Death
Centre) (1997) ISBN 0 712671 11 0